BERNIE AND CHILL

A COLORING BOOK FOR BERNIACS

BERNIE
FOR THE FUTURE
V.P

BERN ALONe

BERNIE'S
BIG ADVENTURE

BERNIE RULES

BERNIE SANDER'S
DAY OFF

The Bernie Kid

THE LITTLE
BERNMAID

bern

The Bernfast Club

MRS.
BERNFIRE

BenWolf

BERN'S WORLD
PREZ
BERNS WORLD

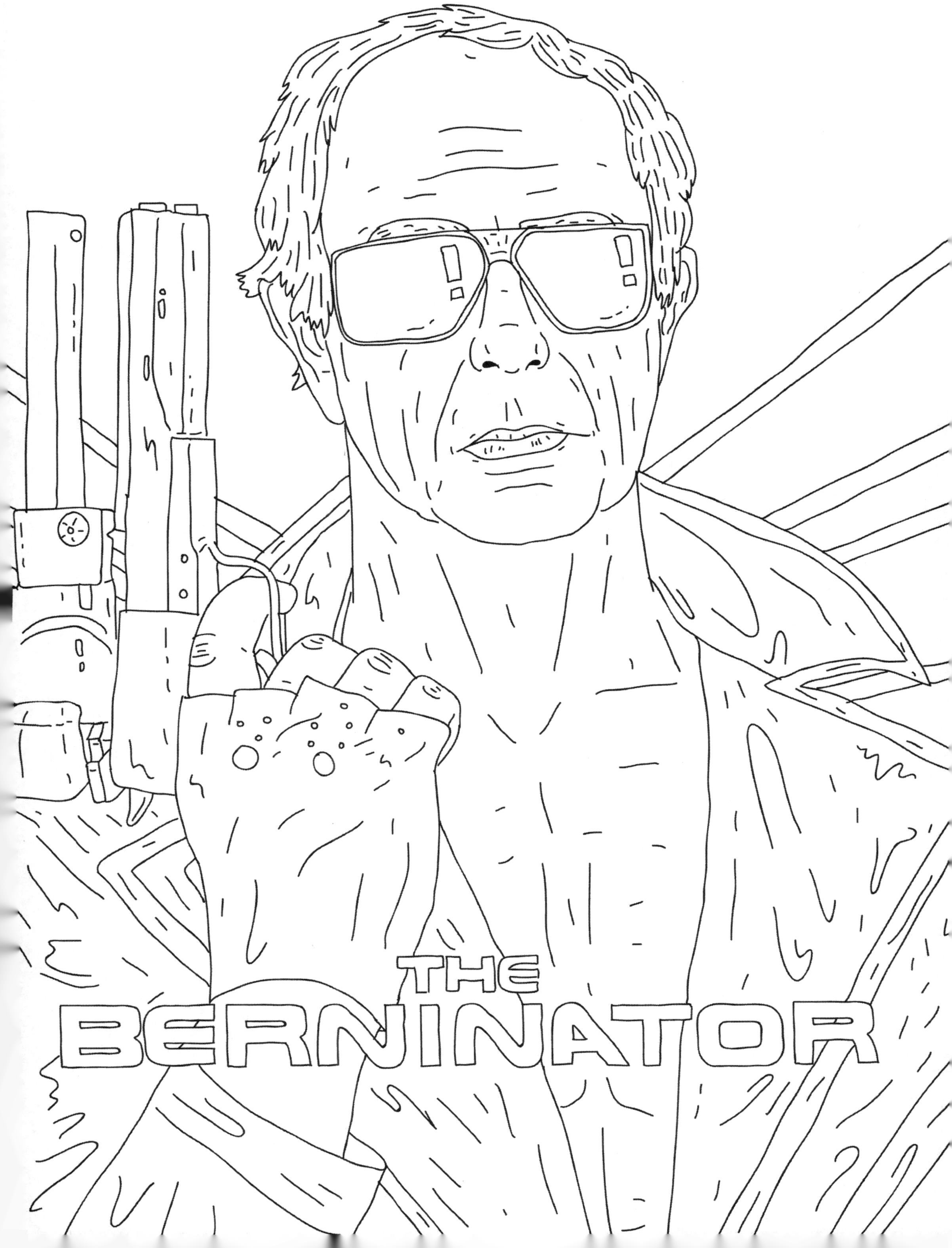
THE
BERNINATOR

32844296R00017

Made in the USA
San Bernardino, CA
16 April 2016